D1270509

G

BIOGRAPHY OF A BEE....

The hive bee, or honeybee, has been known to man for thousands of years. We do not yet know all the facts about bees, but what we do learn each year increases our fascination with these remarkable insects. We know they have an industrious, if somewhat autocratic social structure; that they are capable of communicating with each other and can provide air conditioning for their hives. Here, in simple terms and entertaining illustrations, is what we know of how a bee spends its lifetime.

BIOGRAPHY OF

A

BEE

HARRY SMITH

G. P. Putnam's Sons  New York

CONTENTS....

THE FIRST BEES . . . .

FROM EARLIEST
TIMES...

MENTIONED IN
THE BIBLE

ST. PETER'S,
ROME

The first bees we know of are those whose remains have been found fossilised in amber laid down thousands of years ago when our planet was young. Indeed insects were known to inhabit the earth some 300,000,000 years before man appeared.

In 3300 B.C. the bee was sacred in lower Egypt and its honey and wax used in the ritual burials of the ancient Persian and Egyptian kings. The bodies of dead kings were covered with beeswax to preserve them. These were called "mummies" from the Persian word for wax, mumiya. So you see the bee has been used by man for a long time. You will find references to it in the Bible and later on at school you will learn of Pliny's references to them. If you are ever fortunate enough to visit St. Peter's Church in Rome, be sure to look for the bees carved on the altar by the famous sculptor, Bernini. He did this as a token of gratitude to his patron, Urban VIII, whose family, Barberini, had bees on their coat of arms.

7

THE HIVE AND ITS OCCUPANTS....

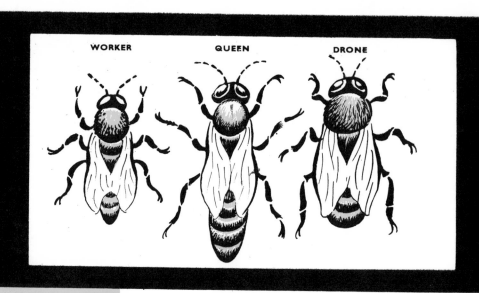

WORKER   QUEEN   DRONE

10,000
SPECIES

TYPES OF BEES WHO
LIVE IN HIVES...

4

SKEP...

Over ten thousand species of bee are known to man, but only 5% of these are social in habit—by that we mean living together. Only four species of these in turn are hive bees and these are called Mellifica, Dorsata, Indica and Florea.

The earliest hives were made of rushes or straw, and in Europe were called skeps. Man has always recognised the importance of beekeeping, not only for his own needs regarding honey but also for the necessity of pollinating the flowers and trees upon which he depends.

However, it was not until the invention of the modern hive in 1851 that it was

8

possible to turn beekeeping into an important business. An average modern hive of today contains between 50,000 and 80,000 bees; most of these are worker bees with one queen and some drones. About a thousand worker bees are lost each day owing to birds, insects and other causes.

THE MODERN BEEHIVE...

POPULATION...

50,000 TO 80,000

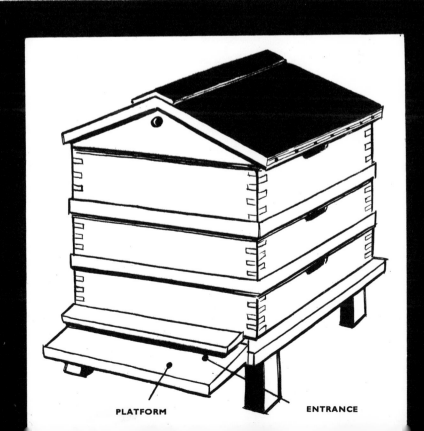

PLATFORM   ENTRANCE

ENEMIES . . . .

MICE...

TOADS...

BIRDS...

DRAGONFLY...

MAN...

A bee's enemies are numerous and include mice, toads, birds and other insects —and, of course, sometimes man. Bees, like many wild creatures, are not aggressive unless frightened or tormented in some way. They are indeed capable of kindness towards each other, as has been noted by observers of their social habits. Food given to a starving colony is distributed all round. If no more food is available, the bees starve together, although the queen, being favoured, is the last to go. On one occasion a worker bee was observed to feed nectar into the mouth of another who had seemingly died of cold. It repeated this act several times until the "dead" bee began to revive. It then helped this bee to its feet and fed it more nectar until it was strong enough to fly off.

Sometimes, of course, their actions appear cruel to us, as in the case of killing off drones at the end of a season. These, however, are actions dictated by instinct for the survival of the community as a whole. An instance of this is the case of a field mouse who raided a hive for honey. The mouse was stung to death and then its body

10

DEFENCE . . . .

A BEE'S STING...

ENTOMBED...

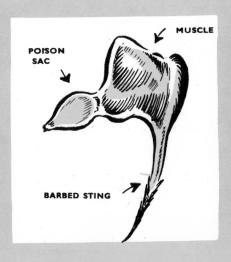

entombed in wax. Since the bees could not have removed the mouse's body, this was their method of preventing it from polluting the hive.

The bee's sting is usually only used in defence, and an attack kills the bee unless it can withdraw its sting. This is not always possible, as on certain things like human skin the barbs on the sting prevent it from being withdrawn. The bee tugs to get away but in doing so tears the sting from its own body and so dies. The muscles attached to the sting, however, continue to pulse for twenty minutes after this, driving it deeper and deeper, and at the same time injecting the poison from the sac. This poison is as potent, drop for drop, as rattlesnake venom.

EQUAL TO RATTLESNAKE VENOM...

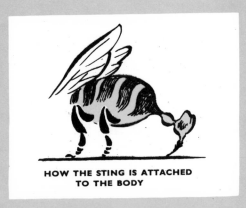

HOW THE STING IS ATTACHED TO THE BODY

MUSCLE

POISON SAC

BARBED STING

SURVIVAL . . . .

CLUSTER

KEEPING WARM...

While a bee's tolerance to radio-activity has proved to be many times that of man, it cannot stand extreme temperatures of cold. If the temperature of a hive drops below 47°F. all the bees will soon die.

One of their methods of creating heat is to form in clusters over the combs. The bees underneath eat and so create a body heat which will keep the outer bees warm. Then they change over with one another and repeat this process over and over again. By this means they can in severe weather raise the inside temperature of a hive to 94°F. In extremely hot weather bees can on the other hand provide air conditioning. This is necessary to keep the hive at a temperature of 93°F. to 95°F., since wax can only be worked at this temperature for

12

making the combs. By fanning their wings rapidly and relaying the air one to another throughout the hive, the inside temperature is kept constant.

AIR CONDITIONING...

WATER

Another method is by bringing in water and pouring it over the combs to keep the hive cool.

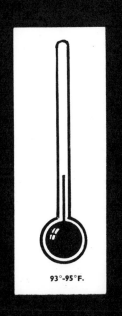

93°-95°F.

WORKER BEES FANNING A HIVE

HOW WAX IS MADE . . . .

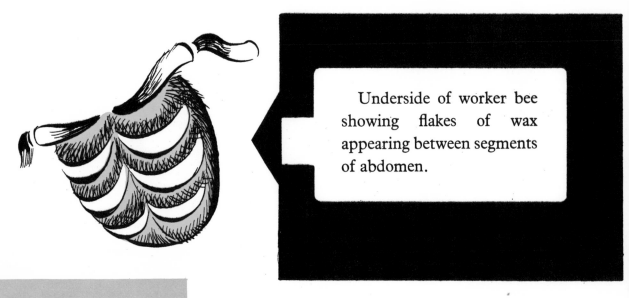

Underside of worker bee showing flakes of wax appearing between segments of abdomen.

WAX PLATES...

ROLLS ITS OWN WAX...

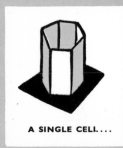

A SINGLE CELL...

The most important building material for bees is of course wax. This is grown by the bee herself, and appears as little plates squeezed out between the segments of her abdomen. These she scrapes off with her legs, and chews them into soft pellets for making the cells in the comb.

The cells can be made in two sizes, the smaller, five to the inch, being used for rearing worker bees and storing pollen. The larger, four to the inch, are used for rearing drones and for the storage of honey and beebread. The walls of a cell are 1/350th of an inch thick.

BUILDING MATERIALS . .

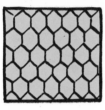

PROPOLIS...

In addition to wax, worker bees will use resin from the buds of poplars and other trees to glue and fasten combs together. This substance is known as propolis.

ONE SQUARE FOOT...

One square foot of comb is obtained from three ounces of wax. This will hold ninety ounces of honey or provide brood cells for 6,000 baby bees. Only at 93°F. to 95°F. is wax ductile—that is soft enough for the bees to work with and make the honey combs.

BEE ROLLING WAX

THE QUEEN . . . .

The picture above shows a queen bee surrounded by her attendants who are so devoted to their sovereign that they caress her continually with their antennae. This, in time, rubs her thorax bare of fuzz.

Only one queen may rule over a hive. When a queen is born, she immediately sets about the task of opening up the other queen cells and killing their occupants.

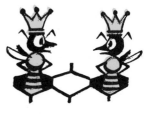

IF TWO QUEENS...

If two queens should happen to be born at the same time then they must fight it out to see who will become ruler of the hive.

THEY WITHDRAW...

Should the two fighting queens reach a stage where they could kill each other simultaneously, then they withdraw and take up a new position. This is in order that one may survive to rule the hive.

The picture on the right shows two queen bees fighting to the death. Each is trying to drive her sting between the plates of her opponent's armour.

TWO QUEENS FIGHT TO THE DEATH

THE DRONE ....

The drone is the playboy of the hive, and since he is born from an unfertilised egg he has therefore no father! The drones hatch in twenty-four days and some hundreds of drones may exist in an average hive and their only purpose seems to be that of mating with the queen.

**DRONE HAS
NO FATHER...**

SUN THEMSELVES...

SPOON FED...

During his lifetime the drone lives off the produce of the hive, and all his life is fed by worker bees. The mouth of a drone is unequipped to make honey or build a comb. He cannot even defend the hive or himself since he has no sting. The drones therefore do nothing but eat, sun themselves, and make occasional practice flights from the hive with young workers.

OCCASIONAL PRACTICE FLIGHTS...

Drones are only tolerated for a few months of each season and at the end of this time when food supplies will be scarcer, the drones are kicked out by the worker bees.

DRONE BEING BUNDLED OUT OF THE HIVE

THE MATING FLIGHT . . . .

When the day comes for the mating flight, all the drones prepare to follow the queen. A queen makes an average of seven such mating flights. Surrounded by such large numbers it is thought that she is less likely to be consumed by birds or dragonflies.

QUEEN IS FAST...

The queen is tremendously fast in the air and in her mating flight spirals upwards followed by all the drones in the hive.

Only the strongest and fastest drone can mate with the queen. This is to ensure that the fittest strain will be born for the future generation. After mating, the drone falls to the ground dead . . . .

...ONLY THE STRONGEST DRONE

SPERMATHECA...

In mating, the queen receives millions of seeds from the drone. These she retains in a special sac inside her body called a spermatheca. Later she will use these seeds to fertilise the eggs she will lay.

THE BIRTH OF A WORKER BEE....

The seeds that the queen receives from the drone are used to fertilise all the eggs that will become female or worker bees. Eggs which develop into males, or drones, are not fertilised. In fact, such eggs can be laid by a queen without ever having mated. Worker or female bees can also when necessary lay eggs but since these too are unfertilised they will only produce more drones.

WORKER BEE SIPPING NECTAR

During her lifetime of three years or more, a queen bee will lay about 15,000 to 18,000 eggs a day. This is over a million eggs, or worker bees. She does not, however, lay eggs during the winter months.

The worker bee is of course the mainstay of the hive and in the following chapters you will see how this hard-working little creature spends her short lifetime of some three weeks.

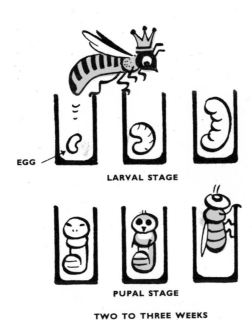

EGG

LARVAL STAGE

PUPAL STAGE

TWO TO THREE WEEKS

EGG LAYING....

THE QUEEN
LAYING
HER EGGS

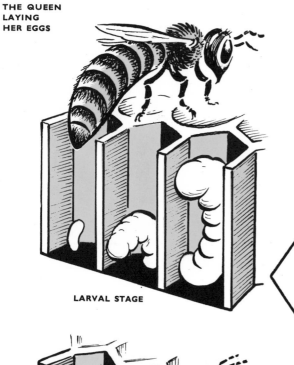

LARVAL STAGE

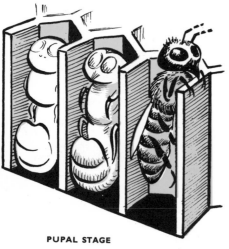

PUPAL STAGE

This cut-away section of the brood cells shows the stages of development from the laying of the egg by the queen to the final hatching of the worker bee. This process takes from two to three weeks.

A BABY BEE

For the first two or three days, the larva is fed with royal jelly, secreted by glands in the head of the nurse or worker bee.

From then on, the worker larvae receive bee-bread—a mixture of pollen and honey.

By enlarging the cell and feeding a three-day-old larva entirely with royal jelly, a queen bee will be produced, but no queen will develop if the larva is more than three days old.

SPECIAL GLAND IN HEAD...

BEEBREAD

JELLY BABIES...

A hive is divided methodically into nurseries and warehouses. Some cells are used for storing pollen or beebread, some for nectar. Others are turned into brood cells, and in the picture above a worker bee is seen feeding the young larvae or baby bees.

The first three weeks of a worker bee's life are devoted to duties in and around the hive. These include cleaning brood cells to receive the queen's eggs, feeding larvae for about eight days, packing pollen or beebread into combs against famine, taking nectar from the field bees and storing it, cleaning refuse from the hive, and guarding the hive against invaders.

CLEANING CELLS...

FEEDING LARVA ...

EXCHANGING NECTAR ...

DEFENDING THE HIVE...

GRADUATION DAY

Finally, the bee graduates to becoming a field worker. . . .

HONEY . . . .

PERSONAL NECTAR

SEGMENTED ABDOMEN

FILLED WITH NECTAR

A bee has two stomachs—one personal and one for carrying nectar. If you look closely at a bee's body, you will find it is divided into segments. When the bee is filled with nectar, the segments are farther apart. In the picture below, you can see two worker bees exchanging nectar. Notice how the abdomen of the one on the left is distended as she receives the nectar.

BEES EXCHANGING NECTAR   NOTICE HOW THE BEE ON THE LEFT IS DISTENDED

The long seven-pronged tongue of a bee is specially adapted to sipping nectar.

A LONG TONGUE...

By swallowing the nectar and regurgitating it, honey is made.

A bee makes an average of ten trips daily for nectar. More trips can be made for pollen, because it is lighter.

TEN TRIPS DAILY...

A bee has been observed to make forty-seven pollen loads in a single day.

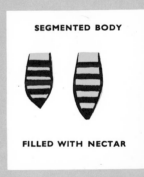

SEGMENTED BODY

FILLED WITH NECTAR

In an eight-week lifetime, a worker bee gathers enough nectar to make about one teaspoonful of honey.

A LIFETIME'S HARVEST...

POLLEN BAGS...

The worker bee has two little bag[s] attached to her hind legs. These are calle[d] Corbicula. By mixing pollen with a littl[e] honey from her stomach, she rolls th[e] mixture into little balls and stuffs ther[m] into the bags or pouches.

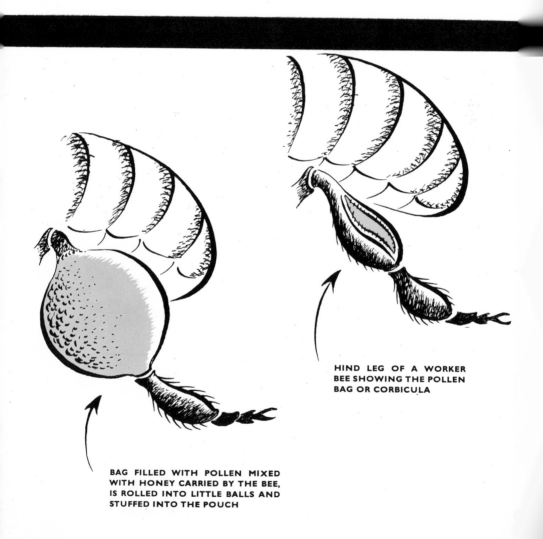

BAG FILLED WITH POLLEN MIXED WITH HONEY CARRIED BY THE BEE, IS ROLLED INTO LITTLE BALLS AND STUFFED INTO THE POUCH

HIND LEG OF A WORKER BEE SHOWING THE POLLEN BAG OR CORBICULA

THE CORBICULA

While a modern aircraft can only carry one-quarter of its own weight in passengers and freight, a worker bee can carry practically its own total weight in pollen and nectar. This it does many more times a day than does the aircraft.

BEE CARRIES ALMOST ITS TOTAL WEIGHT

In addition to carrying materials for its own needs, the bee is also used by nature for the purpose of fertilising plants and flowers. As it goes about its tasks of gathering pollen and nectar, the hairs of the bee become covered with grains of pollen. These are brushed off on to the stigma of flowers, and on the following pages you will see how the plant is then fertilised in this way. Bees usually select just one variety of pollen and just one kind of nectar to turn into honey. This makes bees useful for pollination, since the pollen which does not reach a plant of its own kind goes to waste.

COVERED WITH POLLEN ...

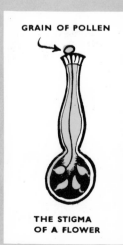

GRAIN OF POLLEN

THE STIGMA OF A FLOWER

31

POLLINATION . . . .

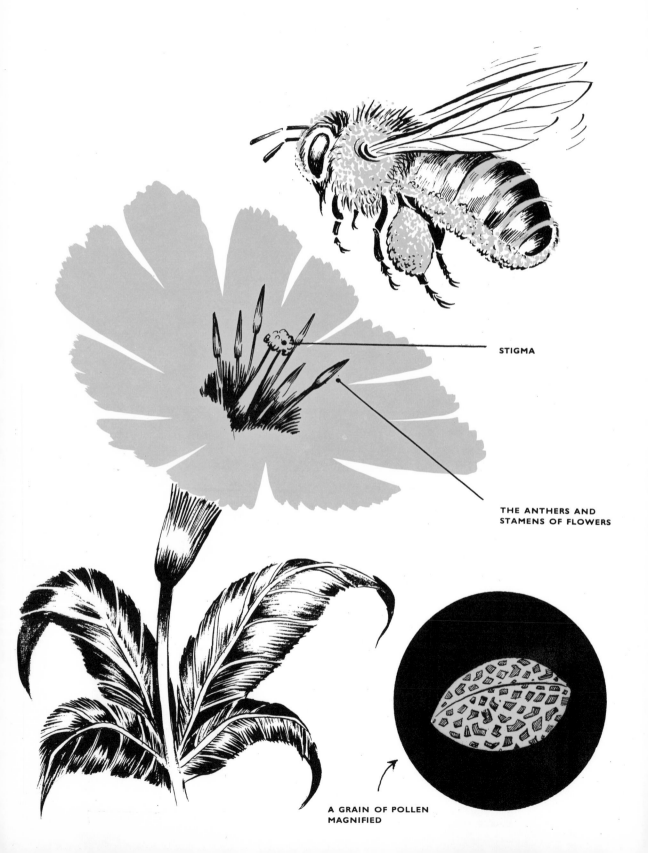

STIGMA

THE ANTHERS AND
STAMENS OF FLOWERS

A GRAIN OF POLLEN
MAGNIFIED

HOW PLANTS ARE FERTILISED
BY THE BEE....

**HAIRS OF BEE ARE
PLUMOSE OR BRANCHED**

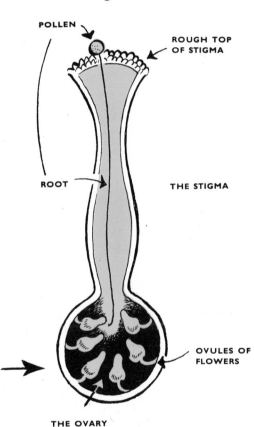

The hairs of a bee are branched, or plumose, so as to retain the pollen grains. The bee combs these off continually by means of the stiff hairs on its legs. In doing so, the pollen grains are transferred to the stigma of flowers.

**A GRAIN OF
POLLEN...**

POLLEN

**ROUGH TOP
OF STIGMA**

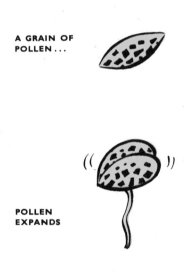

**POLLEN
EXPANDS**

ROOT

THE STIGMA

As the grains of pollen expand, they send roots down the stigma of the plant to fertilise the ovules.

**OVULES OF
FLOWERS**

THE OVARY

Were it not for the bee, plants and flowers would be unable to reproduce. Even the mighty forest elm owes its birth to the bee.

33

**THE MIGHTY
FOREST ELM...**

NAVIGATION AND FLIGHT . . . .

NAVIGATION...

SCENT...

THE DANCE...

The worker bee is an expert navigator. Taking its direction from the sun, it can work out distances, and pass this information on to other bees in the hive. This is done by means of a "dance" or wiggling movement of the body which it performs on return to the hive, in front of the other bees. One observer of these dances has proved that a wiggling movement of 1·2 seconds indicated a distance of some 3,000 feet. In addition to this, the worker bee has a scent gland secreted in its abdomen which it uses to mark flowers and other rich sources of food supplies to the bees.

POLLEN-LADEN BEE EXECUTING DANCE TO OTHER BEES

HOOKS AND EYELETS

CLOSE-UP SHOWING
HOOKS ON EDGE OF
BEE'S WING

It is well known that single wings are necessary for greater speeds in flight, but since the bee also needs to rotate all four wings while gathering nectar and pollen, and on occasion for flying backwards, nature has provided it with wings which can be adapted for all these purposes. When swift flight is required the bee can lock its pairs of wings together by means of little "hooks and eyelets" situated along the leading edge of the hind wing and the anterior edge of the fore wing. At full pressure the wings of a hive bee vibrate at least 250 times per second giving it a top speed of between 10 and 15 miles per hour.

BY MEANS OF
HOOKS...

ALSO
HOVER...

...AND FLY
BACKWARDS

PLASTIC

35

SOME FACTS....

This illustration shows how a bee's wing begins to wear away with continuous flying.

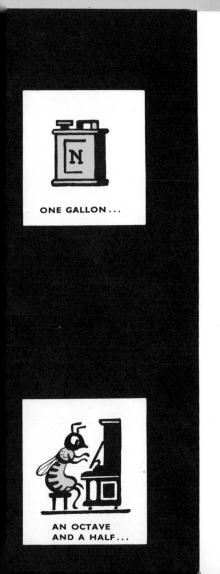

ONE GALLON...

AN OCTAVE AND A HALF...

One observer worked out that a gallon of nectar could provide enough energy for a bee to cruise 4,000,000 miles at 7 miles per hour.

Bees will stop motionless in their tracks when exposed to high intensity sound waves between 600 and 800 cycles per second. That is the pitch of notes an octave and a half above middle C on the piano. Bees' sound receptors are carried in their legs.

The life-span of a field worker bee is four to eight weeks. If it is born late in the season, it may live for six months inside the hive.

WINGS BEGIN TO BREAK

After four to eight weeks' continuous flying, the field worker bee's wings gradually break.

BEE FALLS...

They become smaller and smaller until they can no longer carry the bee and her heavy loads.

DEATH OF A BEE...

THE END

"Biographies" of other
Interesting Creatures

PATCH, A BABY MINK

by Virginia Frances Voight. Illustrated by Steele Savage

PICTA THE PAINTED TURTLE

by Virginia Frances Voight. Illustrated by G. Don Ray

EGGS OF THINGS

by Maxine W. Kumin and Anne Sexton. Illustrated by Leonard Shortall

MORE EGGS OF THINGS

by Maxine W. Kumin and Anne Sexton. Illustrated by Leonard Shortall

BUTTERFLY AND MOTH

by Alice L. Hopf. Illustrated by Jerome Connolly

CHIPPER THE BEAVER

by Ed Dodd. Illustrated by the author

LITTLE BROWN BAT

by Virginia Frances Voight. Illustrated by Earl Thollander

CUFF, A BABY BEAR

by Virginia Frances Voight. Illustrated by Salem Tamer